D0819518

WITHDRAWN
FROM THE RECORDS OF THE
MID-CONTINENT PUBLIC LIBRARY

JB R36WA
Wade, Linda R.
Condolezza Rice

MID-CONTINENT PUBLIC LIBRARY
Blue Ridge Branch
9253 Blue Ridge Blvd. BR
Kansas City, MO 64138

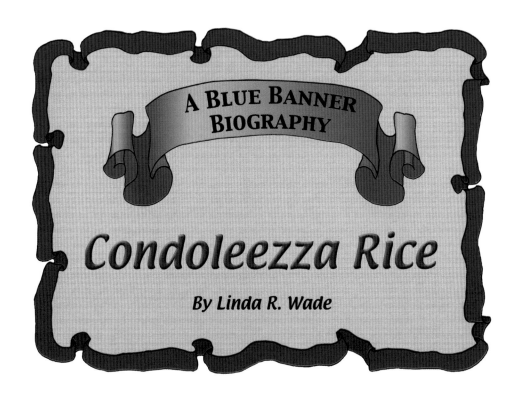

A BLUE BANNER BIOGRAPHY

Condoleezza Rice

By Linda R. Wade

P.O. Box 196
Hockessin, Delaware 19707
Visit us on the web: www.mitchelllane.com
Comments? email us: mitchelllane@mitchelllane.com

MID-CONTINENT PUBLIC LIBRARY
Blue Ridge Branch
9253 Blue Ridge Blvd.
Kansas City, MO 64138

BR

MID-CONTINENT PUBLIC LIBRARY

3 0000 12603304 6

Mitchell Lane
PUBLISHERS

Copyright © 2005 by Mitchell Lane Publishers, Inc. All rights reserved. No part of this book may be reproduced without written permission from the publisher. Printed and bound in the United States of America.

Printing 1   2   3   4   5   6   7   8   9

Blue Banner Biographies

<table>
<tr><td>Alicia Keys</td><td>Allen Iverson</td><td>Avril Lavigne</td></tr>
<tr><td>Beyoncé</td><td>Bow Wow</td><td>Britney Spears</td></tr>
<tr><td>Christina Aguilera</td><td>Christopher Paul Curtis</td><td>Clay Aiken</td></tr>
<tr><td>Condoleezza Rice</td><td>Daniel Radcliffe</td><td>Derek Jeter</td></tr>
<tr><td>Eminem</td><td>Eve</td><td>Ja Rule</td></tr>
<tr><td>Jay-Z</td><td>Jennifer Lopez</td><td>J.K. Rowling</td></tr>
<tr><td>Jodie Foster</td><td>Lance Armstrong</td><td>Mary-Kate and Ashley Olsen</td></tr>
<tr><td>Melissa Gilbert</td><td>Michael Jackson</td><td>Missy Elliott</td></tr>
<tr><td>Nelly</td><td>P. Diddy</td><td>Queen Latifah</td></tr>
<tr><td>Ritchie Valens</td><td>Rita Williams-Garcia</td><td>Ron Howard</td></tr>
<tr><td>Rudy Giuliani</td><td>Sally Field</td><td>Selena</td></tr>
<tr><td>Shirley Temple</td><td></td><td></td></tr>
</table>

Library of Congress Cataloging-in-Publication Data
Wade, Linda R.
    Condoleezza Rice / Linda R. Wade
        p. cm.
    Includes bibliographical reference and index.
    ISBN 1-58415-332-6 (library bound)
    1. Rice, Condoleezza, 1954—Juvenile literature. 2. National Security Council (U.S.)—Biography—Juvenile literature. 3. Presidents—United States—Staff—Biography—Juvenile literature. 4. Large type books. I. Title. II. Series.
    UA23.15.W34 2005
    355'.033073'092—dc22
                                                              2004021878

ABOUT THE AUTHOR: Linda R. Wade is a retired school librarian. She served 23 years in the same school she attended as a child. She has taught writing, both locally and nationally at writing conferences. She received her education from Olivet Nazarene University and Indiana University. She has published 28 books since 1989. She and her husband, Edward, like to travel across the United States visiting their children, historic places, and national parks.

PHOTO CREDITS: Cover: Corbis. p. 4 AP; p. 7 Hulton/Archive; p. 11 Mark Wilson/Getty Images; p. 18 AP; p. 24 Corbis; p. 27 AP

ACKNOWLEDGMENTS: The following story has been thoroughly researched, and to the best of our knowledge, represents a true story. While every possible effort has been made to ensure accuracy, the publisher will not assume liability for damages caused by inaccuracies in the data, and makes no warranty on the accuracy of the information contained herein. This story has not been authorized nor endorsed by Condoleezza Rice.

CONTENTS

Condoleezza Rice became the first woman and second African American to hold the position of the national security advisor. When President Bush was re-elected to a second term, in 2004, he appointed Condoleezza to be secretary of state. She has long been considered President Bush's closest foreign policy advisor and confidant.

Justice is Finally Served

*I*t was quiet on the morning of Sunday, September 15, 1963, in Birmingham, Alabama. Hundreds of parishioners were attending services at the African American 16th Street Baptist Church. In a basement room, 14-year-old Addie Mae Collins helped 11-year-old Denise McNair adjust a colorful sash on her dress. Two other 14-year-olds, Cynthia Wesley and Carol Robertson, watched nearby. Addie's younger sister, 10-year-old Sarah, went into the restroom to wash her hands.

The act would save her life.

At 10:22 a.m., a dynamite bomb explosion rocked the church. The four girls in the basement died instantly, their bodies mangled almost beyond recognition. Cynthia's father could only identify his daughter because of a special ring she wore. Many more people were injured, including Sarah. She has lived the rest of her life with only one eye.

It wasn't the first explosion to rip through Birmingham, but it was the deadliest. The city had been nicknamed "Bombingham" as some white people turned to violence to resist the end of segregation, the policy of racial separation. Black people could not sit at lunch counters with white people. Black people had to ride in the back of buses, drink from marked water fountains, use separate restrooms, even attend different (and usually poorer) schools.

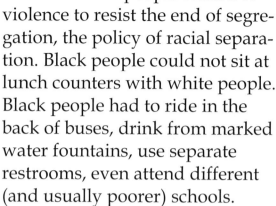

The city had been nicknamed "Bombingham" as some white people turned to violence to resist the end of segregation.

The civil rights movement was trying to end segregation. At that time, Birmingham was widely regarded as its center. Dr. Martin Luther King and other African American leaders were active there, leading protest marches and other non-violent activities.

They were opposed by the public safety commissioner, a man named Eugene Connor. His very fitting nickname was "Bull." Under Connor's orders, police blasted marchers with powerful fire hoses. Vicious police dogs were turned loose. Police attacked demonstrators with clubs, then threw them into jail.

But the violence didn't stop the protesters. The 16th Street Baptist Church was one of the places where local civil rights leaders met regularly to plan strategy. They knew what they were doing was risky. Several anonymous threats during the previous months had targeted the church.

But no threats preceded the September 15 bombing.

People all over the country were outraged. Pictures of the four slain girls were widely published. It became one of the main reasons for the passage of the Civil Rights Act of 1964 and the Voting Rights Act of 1965, which abolished segregation.

Dr. Martin Luther King photographed during a press conference

Authorities began an investigation into the bombing. But it was soon dropped even though an FBI informant reported a taped conversation with someone who bragged that "The boys done a good job on this one. There are a few Negroes now who won't grow up to bother us."

Finally, 14 years later, a man was convicted and sent to prison. In 1988, another who was dying of cancer admitted that he helped plant the bomb. In 2001, a third man was convicted of first-degree murder for the crime. He was sentenced to life imprisonment. And the following year, the man who boasted about the "good job" received the same punishment.

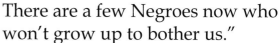

As a young girl Condoleezza lived in Birmingham when the civil rights movement began growing.

This must have come as good news to Condoleezza Rice, an important member of President George W. Bush's inner circle. She was his National Security Advisor.

As a young African American girl, she lived in Birmingham when the civil rights movement began growing. She attended church with her family on the morning of September 15 and was close enough to hear the dreadful explosion.

And she had an even more personal reason for satisfaction.

She had been a friend of Denise McNair.

Growing up in "Bombingham"

*O*n November 14, 1954, Condoleezza Rice was born in Birmingham. She was the only child of John W. and Angelena Ray Rice. Her mother, an accomplished pianist, hoped that her daughter would have a musical career. So she turned to music for a name for her new baby. She thought of the Italian musical term "con dolcezza." It means "with sweetness." Angelena put it altogether and made a new name. Many times it is shortened to Condi.

In many ways, living in Birmingham was anything but sweet. In 1963, Dr. Martin Luther King had been thrown into a Birmingham jail for his part in a protest march. Inside his cell, he wrote that it was "probably the most thoroughly segregated city in the United States."

Condoleezza's parents tried to shield her as much as possible from the discrimination and violence around her. A bomb even went off in her neighborhood. Sometimes her father carried a shotgun and joined other parents on all-night watches because the police could not be depended on to protect them.

She calls her parents "extra-ordinary." Her father was a Presbyterian minister who also taught high school and coached football. Her mother was a music teacher. They taught her confidence and convinced her that she could, as she told *Ebony* (October 1990), "do and be whatever I wanted."

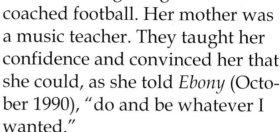

Condoleezza's father was a minister who taught high school and coached football, and her mother was a music teacher.

"My mother was stunningly beautiful," Condoleezza said. "She was tremendously talented. Many of my earliest memories of her are when we would go to shop. I remember how much exposure she gave me to the arts. I remember when I was six she bought me this recording of Aida (a famous opera). She was determined that in segregated Birmingham I would be exposed to culture."

One especially powerful memory came in 1961, when Condoleezza was seven. She found a dress she liked in a department store. She and her mother headed for the dressing rooms so she could try it on. But the rooms were labeled "Whites Only." A saleswoman stood in their path and directed them toward a nearby storage room.

Angelena's response was firm. "My daughter will try on this dress in a dressing room, or I'm not spending my money here," she said.

The salesclerk caved in.

"I remember the woman standing there guarding the door, worried to death she was going to lose her job," Condoleezza recalled.

Long before then, Angelina had taught her daughter how to play the piano. In fact, Condoleezza could read notes before she could read words. She enjoyed playing the music of Bach and Beethoven. And as soon as she was reading words, she had a book in her hands most of the time.

There were few other children around. So much of the time, Condoleezza heard adults talking. Her vocabulary

Condoleezza performs a duet with musician Yo-Yo Ma in 2002. President George W. Bush and first lady Laura Bush attended the event and Bush awarded Ma the National Medal of Arts.

broadened and her teachers said it was "like dealing with a college student because she had an understanding that went beyond her years."

"Condi's always been so focused, ever since she was really, really young," said her aunt, Genoa McPhatter. "She would practice her piano at a certain time without anyone having to remind her."

> "Condi's always been focused, ever since she was really, really young," said her aunt, Genoa McPhatter.

Her father often took summer jobs on college campuses in different parts of the country, and brought his wife and daughter with him. That gave Condoleezza even more respect for the value of an education.

"My parents felt strongly about pushing ahead in education," Condoleezza said. "I had lessons in everything — piano, skating, ballet, and French."

The extra money from these summer jobs helped to pay for all these lessons and the books that Condoleezza always seemed to be reading.

The Rice family was a secure family. They enjoyed each other and had great conversations. Political issues were often topics in their discussions. Their togetherness gave Condoleezza confidence and security. She knew she was safe.

The Family Moves On

When Condoleezza was 11, the Rice family moved to Tuscaloosa, Alabama, about 50 miles away. John Rice had accepted a position as dean of students at Stillman College. It wasn't the first time that Stillman College was important to the Rice family.

In 2000, Condoleezza stood at the podium of the Republication National Convention. George W. Bush had just been nominated for President of the United States. She told this story about her grandfather, a man who was directly descended from slaves.

"George W. Bush would have liked Granddaddy Rice," she said. "He was a poor cotton farmer's son in rural Alabama — but he recognized the importance of education. Around 1918, he decided it was time to get book learning. He asked, in the language of the day, where a colored man could go to college. He was told about little Stillman College, a school about 50 miles away. Granddaddy saved his cotton for tuition and went off to Tuscaloosa.

"After the first year, he ran out of cotton and needed a way to pay for college. Praise be—God gave him one. Grandfather asked how the other boys were staying in school. 'They have what's called a scholarship,' he was told, 'and if you wanted to be a Presbyterian minister, then you could have one, too.'

"Granddaddy Rice said, 'That's just what I had in mind.' And my family has been Presbyterian and college-educated ever since. This is not just my grandfather's story—it is an American story. In America, with education and hard work, it really does not matter where you come from—it matters where you are going."

The family didn't stay long at Stillman. Condoleezza was in the tenth grade when the family moved to Denver, Colorado. John Rice had recently earned an advanced degree from the University of Denver. School officials were so impressed by him that they wanted him to serve as a vice chancellor.

The move was fine with Condoleezza, because she could become a competitive ice skater. Sometimes she

> The family didn't stay long in Stillman. Condoleezza was in the tenth grade when the family moved to Denver.

would get up at 4:30 a.m. to go to practice. It was also the first time that she attended an integrated school.

But even in Denver, she couldn't get away from prejudice. Her guidance counselor told her she wasn't college material. "I had not done very well on the preliminary SAT (Scholastic Aptitude Test) exam," she said in the interview with Ebony. "I remember thinking that the odd thing about it was that [the counselor] had not bothered to check my record. I was a straight-A student in all advanced courses. I was excelling in Latin. I was a figure skater and a piano student. That none of that occurred to her I think was a subtle form of racism."

Because she had skipped both the first and seventh grades, Condoleezza finished high school and enrolled at the University of Denver when she was only 15. Her life course seemed pretty clear. She would become a music major and have a career as a concert pianist.

But things were about to change.

Condoleezza finished high school early and enrolled at the University of Denver when she was only 15.

Change in Plans

When she began her studies at the University of Denver, Condi still enjoyed playing the piano. She practiced many long hours. She even studied one summer at a famous music camp in nearby Aspen.

But soon she began to have misgivings.

It wasn't the first time. She told one interviewer that as a child, "I had been the cute little piano prodigy. But I was getting bored. My mother said, 'You're not old enough, or good enough, to make that decision on your own.'"

Now she was old enough. She admitted to herself that she was not sure she could become a concert pianist. She did not want to become an accompanist, and teaching was out of the question. "I did not want to hear 13-year-olds murder Beethoven," she said. So she left the music program.

She considered English literature. But it was too "squishy." Next she tried government classes. Nothing clicked there either.

Then she met the man who would change the course of her life.

He was Josef Korbel, a former Czech diplomat and a refugee from both the Nazis and the Communists. He was the head of Denver's School of International Relations. Dr. Korbel encouraged Condoleezza to select a career in political science, specializing in international relations.

His classes were fascinating and challenging. "I really adored him," said Rice. "I really did. He's the reason I'm in this field. I loved his course and I loved him. He sort of picked me out as someone who might do this well."

She quickly narrowed her focus to what was then known as the Soviet Union. It consisted of Russia and 15 republics. From then on, it was "Soviet politics, Soviet everything." Condoleezza also learned to speak Russian.

She said, "I was mostly drawn to the study of the Soviet military establishment. While I found the history of war horrific, I also found that I wanted to know more. I

> *Dr. Korbel encouraged Condoleezza to select a career in political science, specializing in international relations.*

studied and learned to think about the unthinkable—
nuclear war and how to prevent it."

Her aunt Genoa happened to be visiting the family on
the day that Condoleezza came home to inform her parents of her change in major studies.

"Her daddy looked at her and said, 'Condoleezza!
Black people don't make money in political science," she
recalled.

But Condoleezza, displaying the firmness that would
soon become one of her main characteristics, replied,
"Music, either."

She went on to graduate magna cum laude (with high
honors) from the University of Denver in 1974. She was

*Condoleezza talks with reporters during a press conference at the White
House.*

only 19. A year later she received her master's degree from the University of Notre Dame. Then at Korbel's suggestion, she returned to the University of Denver to earn her doctorate in international studies in 1981. Her specialty was Soviet politics and culture.

Now, as Dr. Condoleezza Rice, she joined the staff of Stanford University. She was only 26 years old. She was known as a demanding teacher, one who pushed her students to excel and encouraged heated debates. She told a reporter for the New York Times (June 23, 1993), "I tell my students, 'If you find yourself in the company of people who agree with you, you're in the wrong company.'"

Condoleezza joined the staff at Stanford University when she was 26 years old.

She enjoyed teaching and her classes were among the most popular at the school. In just her third year there, she won the Walter J. Gores Award for Excellence in Teaching. She also became a fellow at the Hoover Institute, an internationally known think tank at Stanford, and wrote many articles and two books on Soviet and East European foreign and defense policy.

She appeared to have a secure future as an educator. But soon she would expand her horizons.

CHAPTER 5

From Professor to Politician

By this point, her political views were firmly established. Though she voted for Democrat Jimmy Carter in the 1976 presidential election, she quickly lost faith in him.

She thought that he didn't deal very effectively with the Soviet Union. The last straw came when Carter didn't allow the U.S. team to go to the 1980 Olympics, which were held in Moscow.

"I thought it was weak," she said.

So she became a Republican.

"The first Republican I knew was my father and he is still the Republican I most admire," Condoleezza said when she addressed the 2000 Republican Convention. "He joined our party because the Democrats in the Alabama of 1952 would not register him to vote. My father has never forgotten that day, and neither have I. However, I joined for a different reason. I found a party that sees me as an individual, not as part of a group. I found a party that puts family first. I found a party that has love of liberty at its core. And I found a party that believes that peace begins with strength."

She happily supported Carter's replacement as President, Ronald Reagan. He was everything that Carter was not. "His (Reagan's) great strength was that he had a couple of clear principles that he held to," she said. "He mobilized the power of the United States and hit on a rollback strategy that challenged the Soviets."

In 1987 she was asked to serve as an advisor to the Joint Chiefs of Staff on strategic nuclear policy. She also briefed Air Force generals on strategy and force posture in the Soviet military. Then she traveled to Bulgaria to speak to Soviet officials and diplomats on arms control policy.

In 1988, Rice received a call from Madeleine Albright. She was Dr. Korbel's daughter and an important Democrat who would eventually become President Bill Clinton's secretary of state. The two women had never met. Albright assumed that Condoleezza was a Democrat because of Dr. Korbel's influence and because she had come from segregated Birmingham. She suggested that

> *Condoleezza served as an advisor to the Joint Chiefs of Staff on strategic nuclear policy.*

the two women work together to help elect Michael Dukakis, the governor of Massachusetts who was the Democratic candidate for the presidency that year.

There was a long silence.

Then Condoleezza finally replied, "Madeleine, I don't know how to tell you this. I'm a Republican."

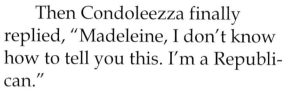

Condoleezza was the highest-ranking African American woman on the National Security Council.

In the following year, Condoleezza received a call she appreciated a lot more. It was from President George Herbert Walker Bush. He needed her expertise and knowledge on Soviet affairs. She joined the National Security Council at the personal request of Brent Scowcroft, the National Security Advisor at that time. During her tenure, she was the highest-ranking African American woman on the Council. She quickly advanced from her position of director to senior director of Soviet and Eastern Affairs.

President Bush took her to a meeting with Mikhail Gorbachev, the Soviet leader. He introduced her by saying, "This is Condoleezza Rice. She tells me everything I know about the Soviet Union."

The young lady who entered the University of Denver planning to become a concert pianist had changed into a dynamic stateswoman.

Back to Stanford

I t was an exciting time to be in Washington, D.C. So many changes were taking place. The Berlin Wall had come down so that people living in Communist East Germany could now move freely to the West. Then the Soviet Union dissolved. The United States enlisted Russia as an ally in the war against Iraq in the Persian Gulf.

In 1991, after two years in Washington, Condoleezza Rice headed back to Stanford. Two years later, she received the School of Humanities and Sciences Dean's Award for Distinguished Teaching. And on September 1 that year, she became the university's provost. That's the second-highest job on the campus, responsible for a budget of one and a half billion dollars, 1,400 professors and 14,000 students.

At 38, she was the youngest person ever named to that position. It caused a controversy on campus because she was promoted over many people who had expected to get the job. But even people who opposed her agree that she did an outstanding job.

Normally the position of provost is the steppingstone to the next level, which is to become president of a university. But Condoleezza said she had no interest in doing that. She wanted to "get back to my roots as a Russianist."

During this time, she also became involved in many professional and community activities. Children have

Condoleezza photographed during an appearance on a German television show.

always been one of her concerns. She helped found the Center for New Generation, an after-school enrichment program for kids in East Palo Alto, California. She became Vice President of the Boys and Girls Club of the Peninsula.

Soon after stepping down as provost, she began helping then-Texas Governor George W. Bush prepare for his presidential campaign. She stayed current with all the happenings in other countries. Each day she met with him and reported on world events. She offered suggestions on dealing with foreign countries.

She helped found the Center for New Generation, an after-school enrichment program for kids.

National Security Advisor

*I*n December, 2000, President-Elect Bush appointed Condoleezza as the next National Security Advisor. When he took the oath of office the following January, she became the first woman and second African American (after Colin Powell) to hold that position, which coordinates American policy toward the rest of the globe.

She quickly acquired a reputation as tough, decisive, and extremely self-confident, someone who doesn't pull punches. Yet, her gentle smile and winning personality often eased the strain of a tough negotiating session.

As National Security Advisor, she became accustomed to long workdays. They often began early and didn't end until well into the evening. They included daily meetings with President Bush and attending every Cabinet meeting. She often saw visitors from other countries.

Condoleezza became a key player in the Bush inner circle after the terrorist attacks on September 11, 2001. She helped issue an ultimatum to the Taliban, the ruling party in Afghanistan who had sheltered the terrorists. She approved military action against them.

She enjoyed a good working relationship with President Bush. He described her as the person who "can explain to me foreign policy matters in a way I can understand."

Condoleezza enjoys a good working relationship with President George W. Bush.

In *Biography Magazine*, she said, "Family and faith are important to both of us. We also have a similar sense of humor. We find a lot of the same things funny. Both of us are devoted sports people. And what I really love about the President is that he has a perspective about life that doesn't always make you the center of everything. I've never very much taken to people who are puffed up with their own importance."

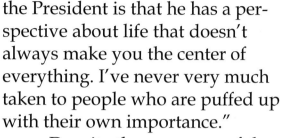

Despite the pressures of the job, she has a personal life as well. She has always enjoyed working out.

Despite the pressures of the job, she has a personal life as well. She has always enjoyed lifting weights and working out. Finding time to play the piano is important too.

She is also a big sports fan, probably because of her father's influence. She loves tennis and watching both college and professional football. In fact, she has sometimes said that her dream job is commissioner of the National Football League. When she met Paul Tagliabue, the commissioner at that time, he told her that he had heard she was angling for his job.

"Not to worry," she answered, "but let me know when you're thinking of retiring."

From the beginning Condoleezza's parents gave her strength and encouragement. The family took a trip to Washington D.C. when she was only 10 years old. As

Condoleezza stared at the White House through its gate she told her father, "One day, I'll be in that house."

Condoleezza's mother died of cancer in 1985, far too soon to see her prophecy come true. Her father died of heart disease in late 2000. On his deathbed he learned that President-elect Bush had just appointed his daughter to be national security advisor.

After President Bush was re-elected in 2004 for a second term, Condoleezza was appointed secretary of state. She was the first African American woman and only the second woman to hold the position.

"The secretary of state is America's face to the world and in Dr. Rice the world will see the strength, grace and decency of our country, " President Bush said.

Condoleezza sums her life up this way. "I've enjoyed a wonderful life, a great life, graced by ideal parents. I have a very, very powerful faith in God. I'm a really religious person, and I don't believe that I was put on this earth to be sour, so I'm eternally optimistic about things."

Condoleezza predicted at a young age that some day she'd be in the White House.

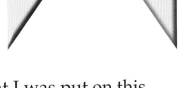

CHRONOLOGY

1954	Born on November 14 in Birmingham, Alabama, to John W. and Angelena Rice
1958	Begins taking piano lessons
1970	Enters University of Denver at the age of 15
1974	Graduates from University of Denver at the age of 19
1975	Receives masters degree from Notre Dame University
1981	Receives Ph.D. degree from the University of Denver; joins faculty of Stanford University
1984	Publishes first book; receives Walter J. Gores Award for Excellence in Teaching at Stanford
1987	Serves as advisor to the Joint Chiefs of Staff on strategic nuclear policy
1989	Becomes Director of Soviet and East European Affairs on National Security Council
1991	Returns to Stanford; awarded honorary doctorate from Morehouse College
1992	Speaks at Republican National Convention
1993	Receives the School of Humanities and Sciences Dean's Award for Distinguished Teaching; becomes provost at Stanford
1994	Receives honorary doctorate from University of Alabama
1995	Receives honorary doctorate from Notre Dame
2000	Makes speech at Republican National Convention
2001	Becomes national security advisor to President George W. Bush

2002   Active in President Bush's war on terrorism and in
        demand for new Palestinian leadership
2003   Advises American public of President Bush's war
        with Iraq; awarded honorary doctorate from
        Mississippi College School of Law
2004   Awarded honorary doctorate from University of
        Louisville and Michigan State. Appointed secretary of
        state during President George W. Bush's second term
        as President.

Websites
www-hoover.stanford.edu/bios/rice.html

Books

Cunningham, Kevin. *Condoleezza Rice: Educator and Presidential Adviser (Journey to Freedom)*. Chanhassen, MN: Child's World, 2005.

Ditchfield, Christin. *Condoleezza Rice: National Security Advisor (Great Life Stories)*. Danbury, CT: Franklin Watts 2003.

Felix, Antonia. *Condi: The Condoleezza Rice Story*. New York: Newmarket Press, 2002.

Wade, Mary Dodson. *Condoleezza Rice: Being the Best*. Minneapolis: Millbrook Press, 2003.

INDEX